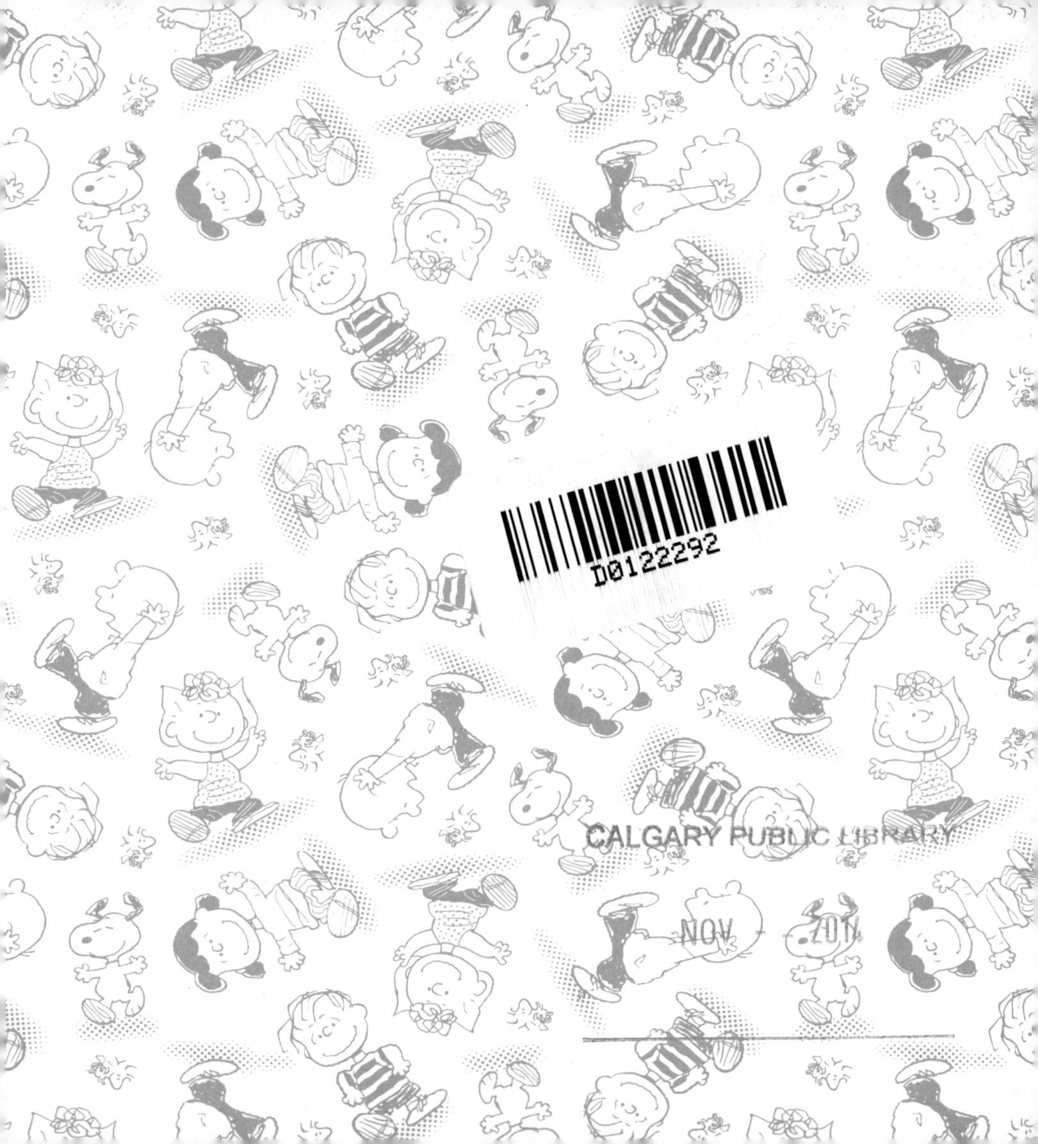

PEANUTS

GUIDE TO LIFE

PEANUTS

GUIDE TO LIFE

by Charles M. Schulz

Wit and Wisdom from the World's
Best-Loved Cartoon Characters

Foreword by Andy Cohen

RUNNING PRESS
PHILADELPHIA · LONDON

© 2004, 2014 by Peanuts Worldwide LLC
Published by Running Press,
A Member of the Perseus Books Group

Printed in China

Books published by Running Press are available at special discounts for bulk purchases
in the United States by corporations, institutions, and other organizations.
For more information, please contact the Special Markets Department at the
Perseus Books Group, 2300 Chestnut Street, Suite 200, Philadelphia, PA 19103, or
call (800) 810-4145, ext. 5000, or e-mail special.markets@perseusbooks.com.

ISBN 978-0-7624-5432-7
Library of Congress Control Number: 2013954662

9   8   7   6   5   4   3   2   1
Digit on the right indicates the number of this printing

Cover design by Melissa Gerber
Edited by Zachary Leibman
Typography: Archer, Archive Antique Extended,
and Trade Gothic

Running Press Book Publishers
2300 Chestnut Street
Philadelphia, PA 19103-4371

Visit us on the web!
www.runningpress.com

TABLE OF CONTENTS

FOREWORD

"As soon as a child is born, he or she
should be issued a dog and a banjo."

—Charlie Brown

When I was born, the dog I was issued was Snoopy.
My stuffed Snoopy came with me pretty much
everywhere I went. He was cute. He slept with me.
He hugged me. He made me smile. As long as Snoopy was
there, he made me feel like I was home.

Before I went to bed at night my dad would come tuck me
in and hold Snoopy to his ear, repeating to me the things that
Snoopy told him about me. Of course I believed that Snoopy
could talk and I wanted to hear what he had to say. I found out
later he had *a lot* to say . . .

If my mom's omnipresent *Peanuts* calendar wasn't close, I
could tell what time of year it was by what *Peanuts* special was

on TV. It seemed like Snoopy and the gang were all around me. I liked to draw Snoopy (I still find myself doodling his head and tummy while daydreaming in meetings) and Charlie Brown (especially his shirt and weird shoes). As I got older, I got really plugged into the comic strip and started digesting something larger than just a cartoon.

What did I learn about life from a dog and a bunch of kids? A lot.

Snoopy, Charlie Brown, Linus, Lucy, Sally, and the whole gang can teach us pretty much everything we need to know about how to behave and we have Charles Schulz to thank for that. In my estimation, the cartoonist deserves an A+ in philosophy; his simple wisdom captivated hundreds of millions of fans around the world and somehow gives all of us permission to feel good about searching for deeper meaning around us.

His messages are simple and universal: Believe in yourself ("Who cares what other people think?"—Sally); find happiness in the little things around you; be decent, self-reliant, and optimistic ("Keep looking up . . . that's the secret of life."—Snoopy);

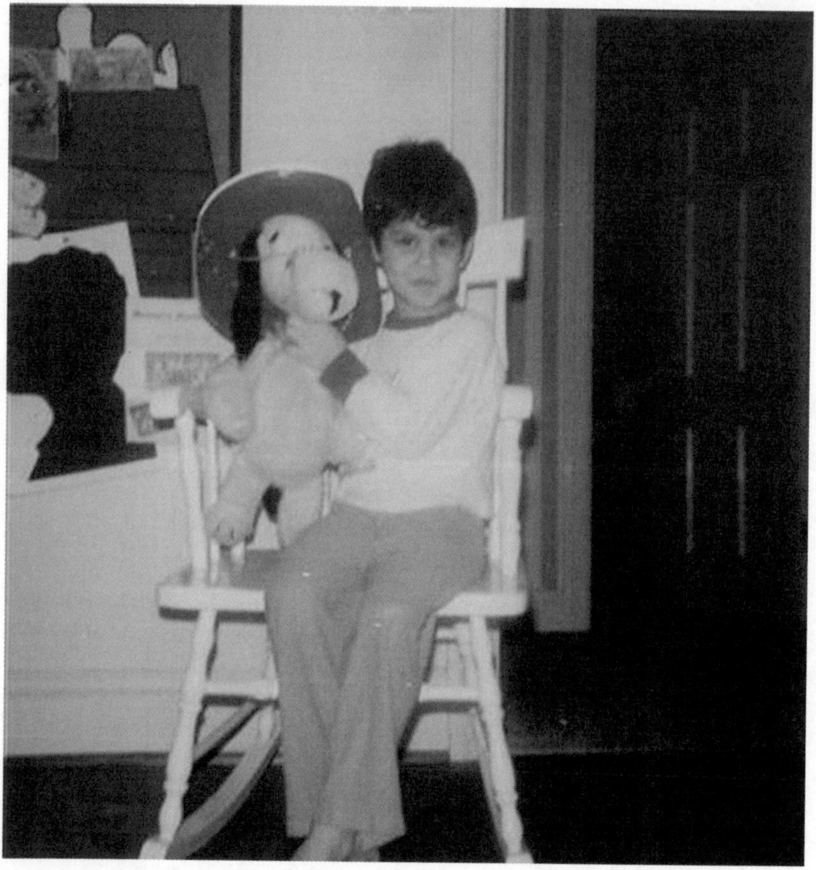

work hard ("No one need ever be ashamed of fingernails made dirty by a hard day's work."—Linus); and above all, allow yourself to *love* (even though Lucy points out, "It's amazing how stupid you can be when you're in love.").

I don't know how he got away with it, but Schulz had an uncanny ability to simultaneously present joy and melancholy all at once. And that melancholy is part of what makes his work so prescient for me. Schulz made it okay to feel kind of blah every once in a while. That's just part of life. (And by the way, how "blah" can you feel when Snoopy's outside lying on his doghouse?)

Peanuts Guide to Life is a collection of some of Schulz' most simple and entertaining philosophy. It is a perfect roadmap for us all to navigate humanity with dignity and fun.

Oh, and by the way, happiness IS a warm puppy!

Andy Cohen
New York City, 2013

LIFE
PHILOSOPHY

THIS IS MY REPORT ON HOW TO LIVE..
THEY SAY THE BEST WAY IS JUST TO LIVE ONE DAY AT A TIME..
IF YOU TRY TO LIVE SEVEN DAYS AT A TIME, THE WEEK WILL BE OVER BEFORE YOU KNOW IT..
© 1990 United Feature Syndicate, Inc.
2-16
SCHULZ

"Life is like an ice cream cone . . .
you have to learn to lick it!"

Charlie Brown

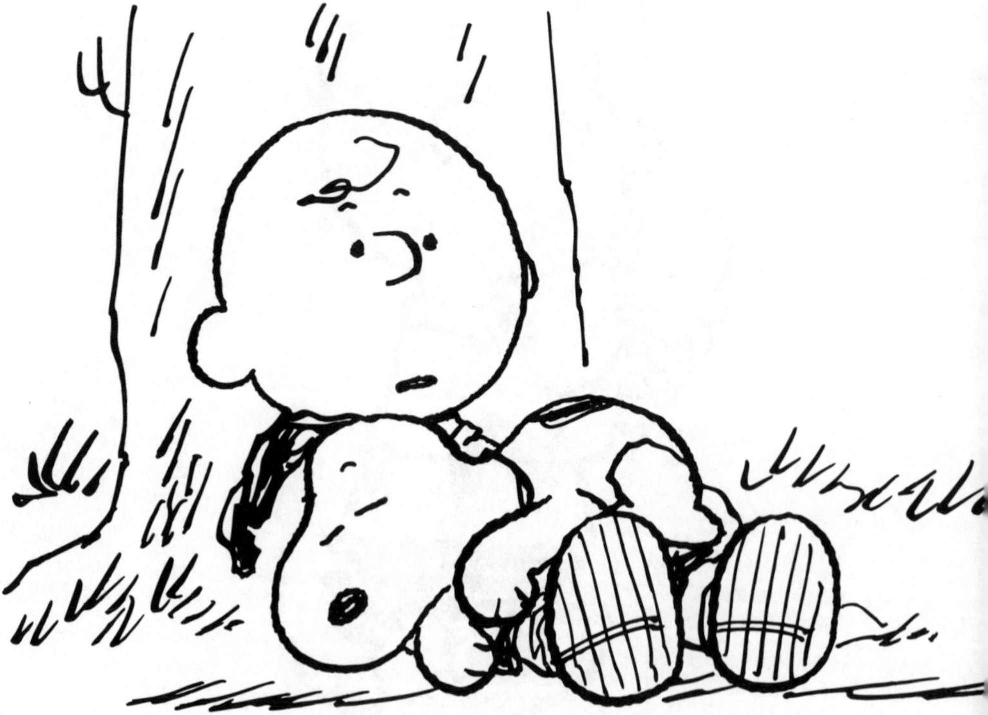

"As soon as a child is born,
he or she should be issued
a dog and a banjo . . ."

Charlie Brown

"They say if you become a better person,
you'll have a better life . . ."

Charlie Brown

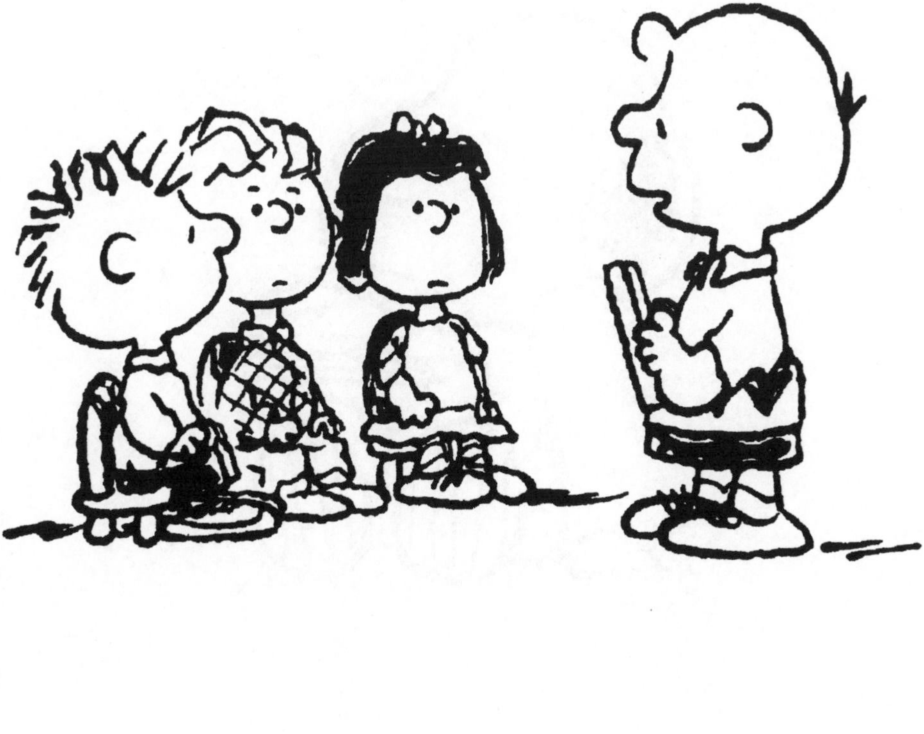

"If you try to be a better dog,
sometimes you get an
extra cookie ..."

Snoopy

"I have a philosophy that has been refined in the fires of hardship and struggle . . . 'Live and let live!'"

Lucy

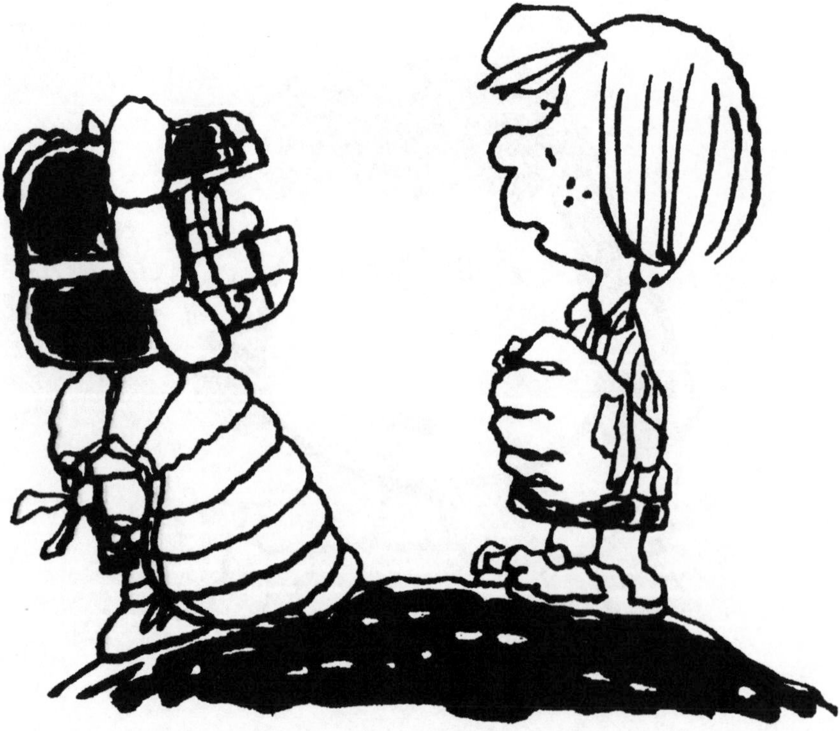

"A life should be planned
inning by inning."

Peppermint Patty

CONFIDENCE

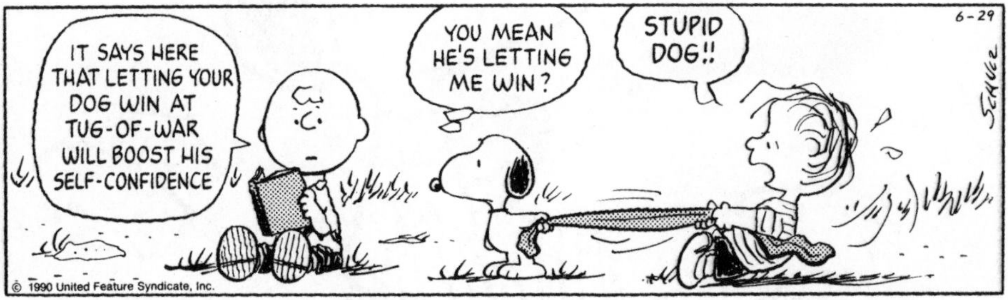
6-29
IT SAYS HERE THAT LETTING YOUR DOG WIN AT TUG-OF-WAR WILL BOOST HIS SELF-CONFIDENCE
YOU MEAN HE'S LETTING ME WIN?
STUPID DOG!!
SCHULZ
© 1990 United Feature Syndicate, Inc.

"It's better to live one day as a lion
than a dozen years as a sheep."

Snoopy

"If everybody agreed with ME, they'd all be right!"

Lucy

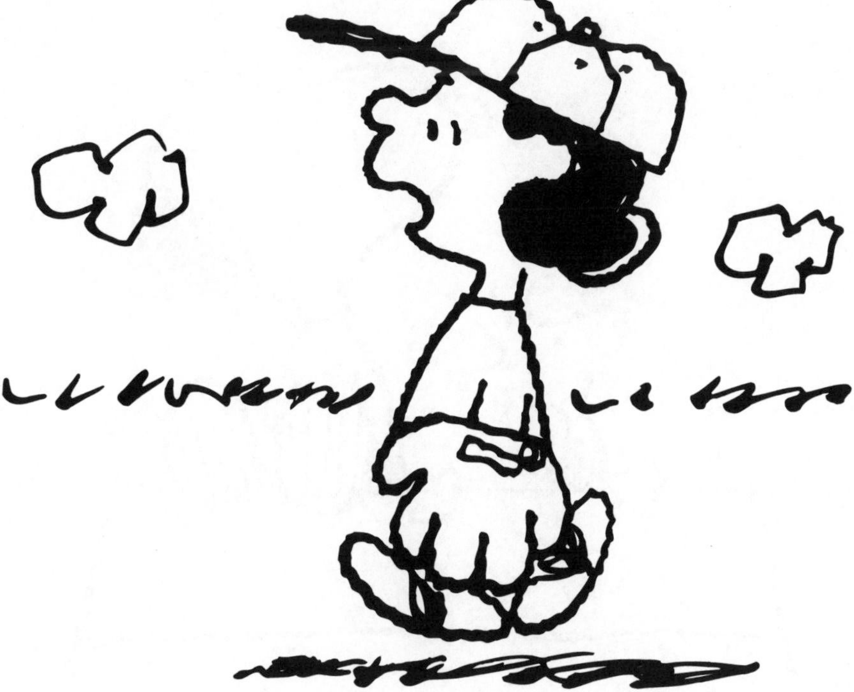

"Keep looking up . . .
That's the secret of life . . ."

Snoopy

"When you go some place nice,
you should always shine your feet!"

Snoopy

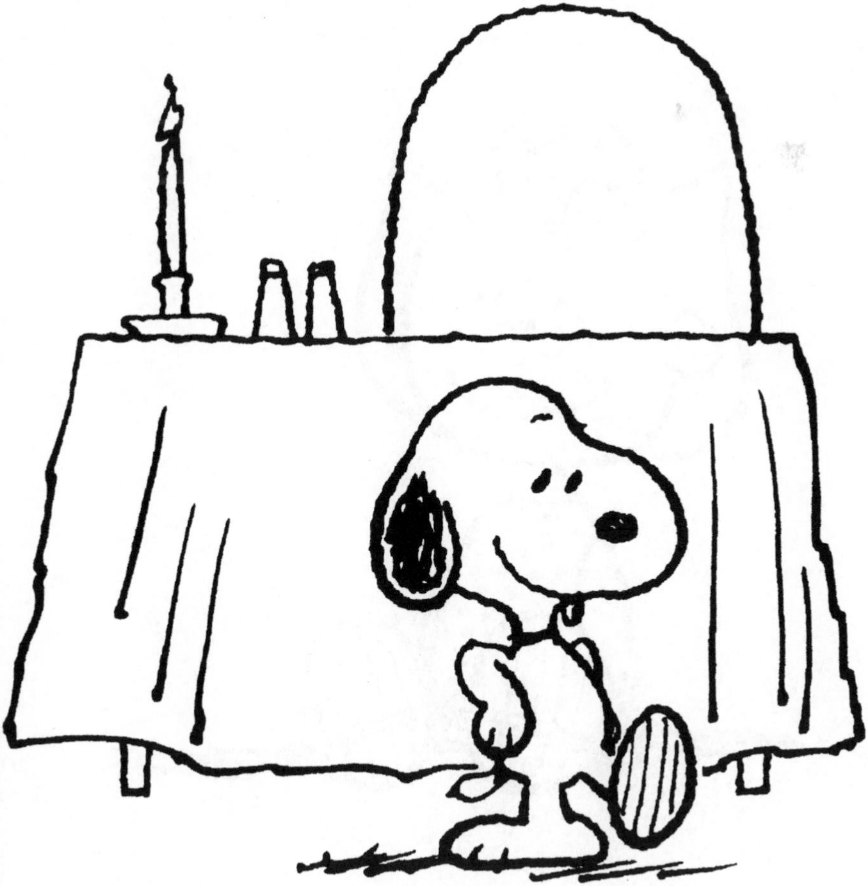

"'All is well'…
That's my new philosophy…"

Sally

SELF-CARE

I SIGNED UP FOR A SUMMER READING PROGRAM AT THE LIBRARY...
GOD DIDN'T MAKE THE SUN FOR YOU TO SIT IN THE LIBRARY, MARCIE
YOU KNOW MORE ABOUT THEOLOGY THAN I THOUGHT, SIR
6/6
© 1990 United Feature Syndicate, Inc.

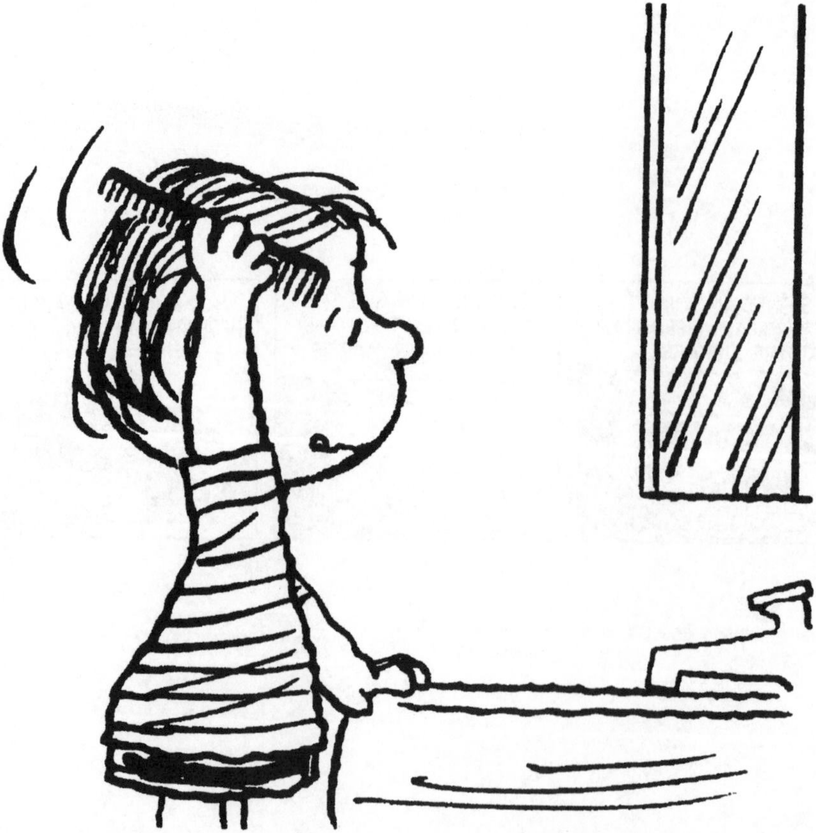

"Sometimes all we need
is a little pampering to
help us feel better . . ."

Linus

"Insulate the ol' attic!"

Snoopy

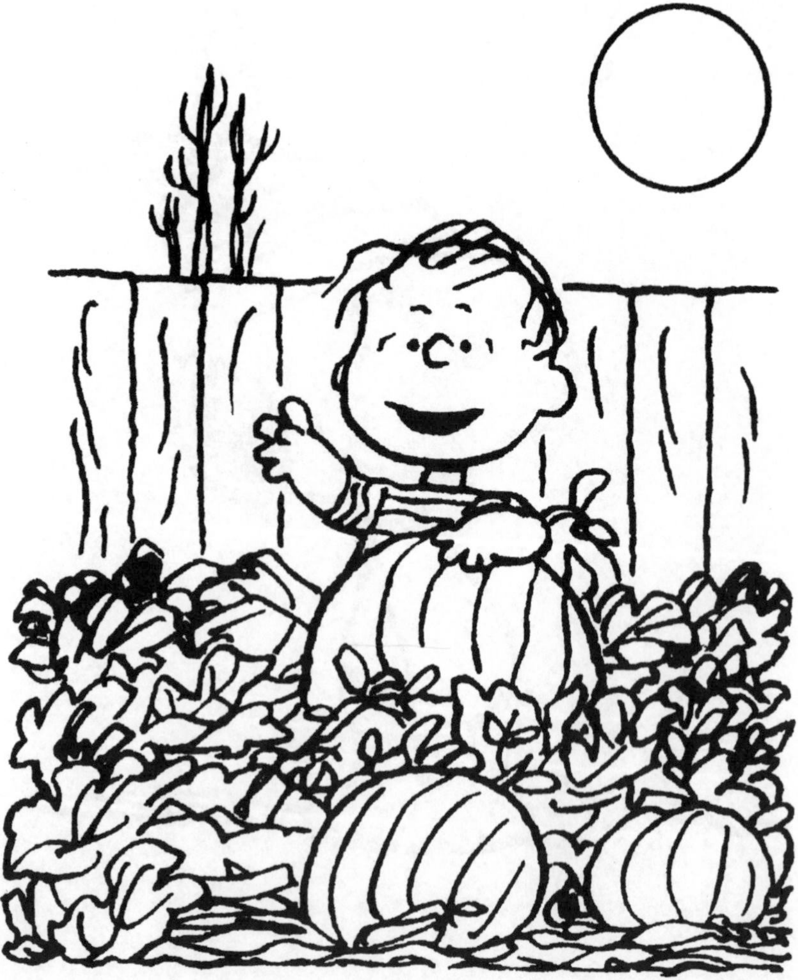

"Most psychiatrists agree that sitting in a pumpkin patch is excellent therapy for a troubled mind!"

Linus

SELF-RELIANCE

I'VE NEVER BEEN ABLE TO UNDERSTAND HOW LITTLE KIDS LEARN TO TIE THEIR SHOES...
© 1990 United Feature Syndicate, Inc.
IT'S REALLY EASY... AFTER A WHILE IT BECOMES ALMOST AUTOMATIC....
7-2
UNLESS YOU THINK ABOUT IT!!!
SCHULZ

"If you want something done right, you should do it yourself!"

Snoopy

"Well from now on, Linus,
think for yourself… Don't take
any advice from anyone!"

Charlie Brown

"Who cares what
other people think?"

Sally

"You can't believe everything you hear, you know…"

Schroeder

PEOPLE SKILLS

WHEN YOUR CLIENTS COME IN FOR AN INTERVIEW, DO YOU DO ANYTHING SPECIAL TO PUT THEM AT EASE?
9-1
© 1990 United Feature Syndicate, Inc.
I GIVE THEM A BALLOON
SCHULZ

"If you can't beat 'em,
cooperate 'em to death!"

Charlie Brown

"In first-aid class I learned
that if you have offended someone,
the best treatment is to
apologize immediately…"

Marcie

"The average dad needs
lots of encouragement."

Charlie Brown

"When you get a compliment,
all you have to say is 'thank you.'"

Classmate talking to Rerun

PRUDENCE

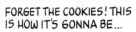

FORGET THE COOKIES! THIS IS HOW IT'S GONNA BE...
© 1990 United Feature Syndicate, Inc.
EITHER YOU GIVE ME THAT BLANKET OR I TIE YOUR EARS TOGETHER, TAKE YOU UP TO THIRTY THOUSAND FEET AND DROP YOU INTO THE GRAND CANYON!
6-9
OH? IS THIS YOUR BLANKET?
SCHULZ

"It's a mistake to try to avoid
the unpleasant things in life . . .
But I'm beginning to consider it . . ."

Charlie Brown

"I've got to stop this business
of talking without thinking . . ."

Linus

"A person has to be careful
about things he might regret
years from now."

Linus

"There's no sense in doing a lot of barking if you don't really have anything to say."

Snoopy

WISDOM

FROM NOW ON I INTEND TO MOVE THROUGH LIFE WITH TOTAL SERENITY...
1-4-91
DO YOU REALLY THINK YOU CAN?
© 1990 United Feature Syndicate, Inc.
WELL, WHY NOT?
SCHULZ

"I have observed that whenever you try to hit somebody, there is a tendency for them to try to hit you back."

Charlie Brown

"Whenever it's one man against an institution, there is always a tendency for the institution to win!"

Charlie Brown

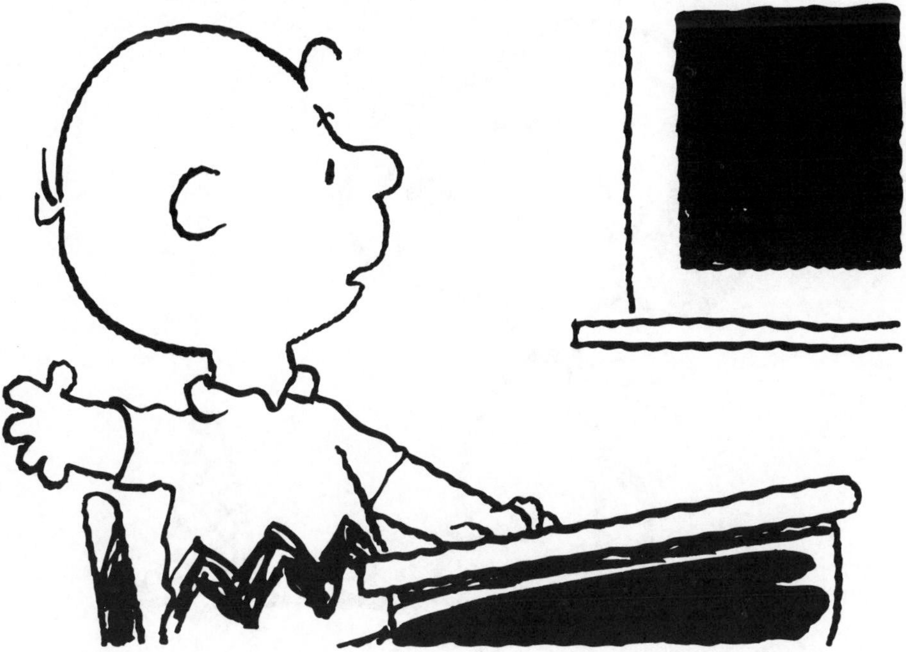

"Never try to lick ice cream
off a hot sidewalk!"

Snoopy

"Never try to eat a sugar-sandwich
on a windy day!"

Charlie Brown

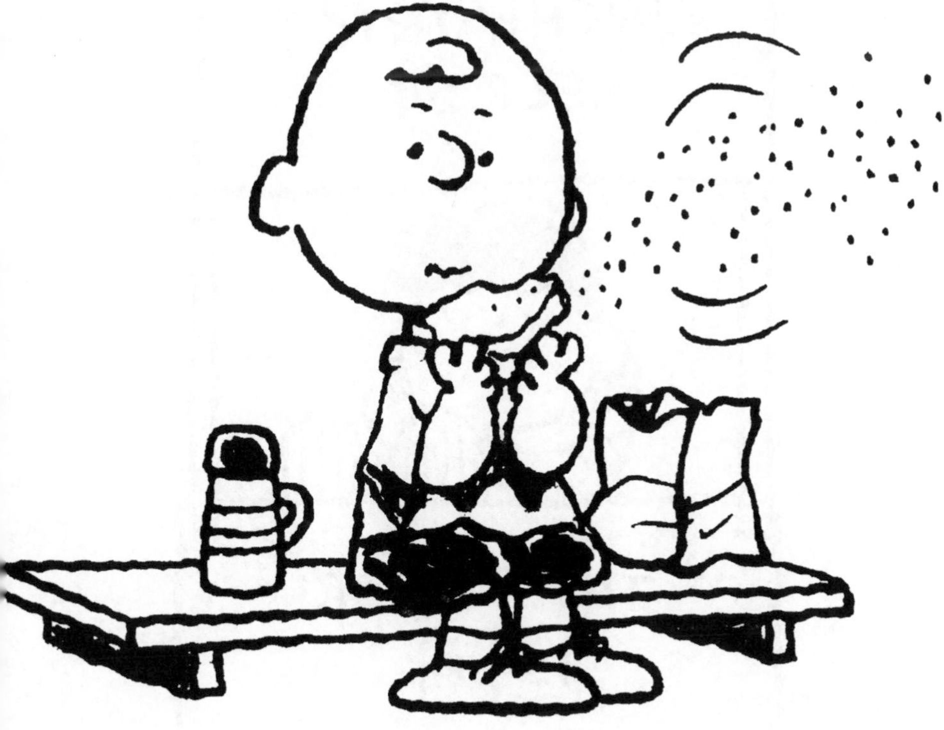

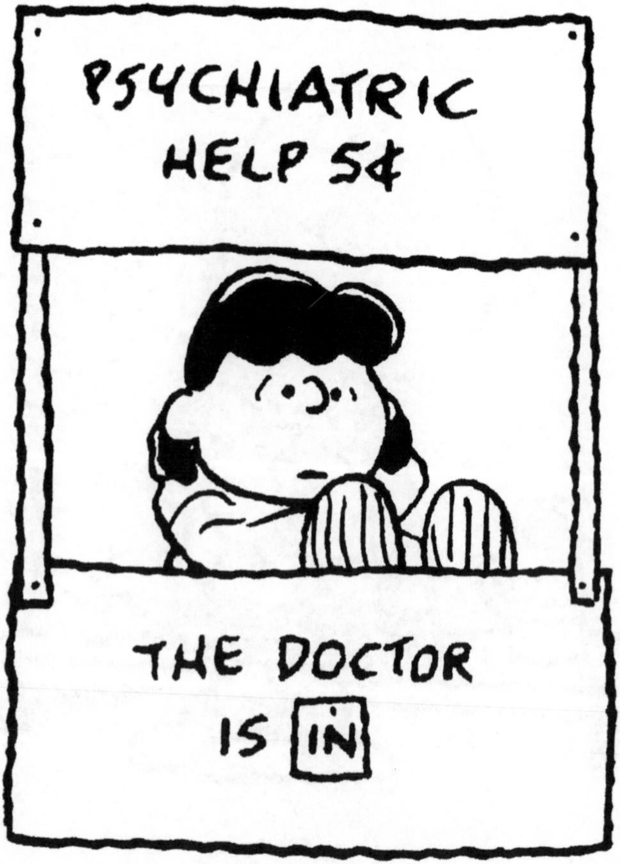
PSYCHIATRIC HELP 5¢
THE DOCTOR IS IN

"Never take any advice that you can understand . . . it can't possibly be any good!"

Lucy

"Never jump into a pile of leaves holding a wet sucker!"

Linus

EFFORT

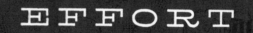

3-26
THAT'S RIGHT.. IT'S YOUR JOB TO TELL EVERYONE THAT SPRING HAS COME..
© 1990 United Feature Syndicate, Inc.
BUT NOT IN DETAIL!
SCHULZ

"If you don't play every day,
you lose that fine edge . . ."

Snoopy

"Some of my best term papers have been written before breakfast!"

Sally

"No one need ever be ashamed
of fingernails made dirty by
a hard day's work."

Linus

" John Ruskin once wrote
'the best grace is the consciousness
that we have earned our dinner.'"

Linus

"Good cookies come
when they're called."

Snoopy

LOVE

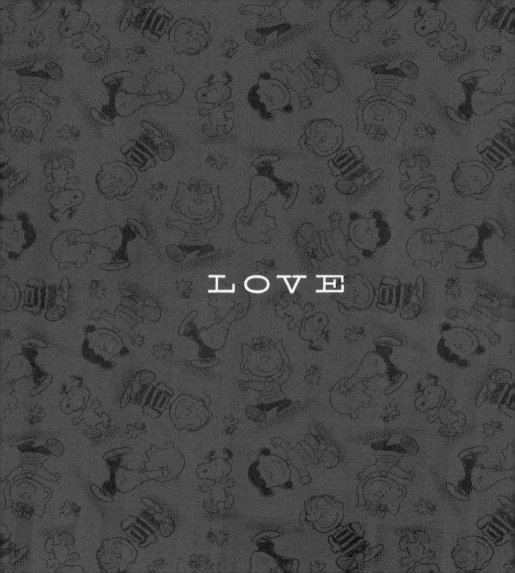

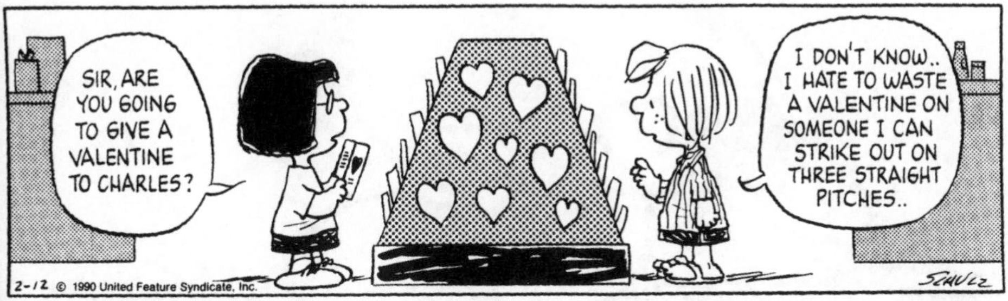
SIR, ARE YOU GOING TO GIVE A VALENTINE TO CHARLES?
I DON'T KNOW.. I HATE TO WASTE A VALENTINE ON SOMEONE I CAN STRIKE OUT ON THREE STRAIGHT PITCHES..
2-12 © 1990 United Feature Syndicate, Inc.
SCHULZ

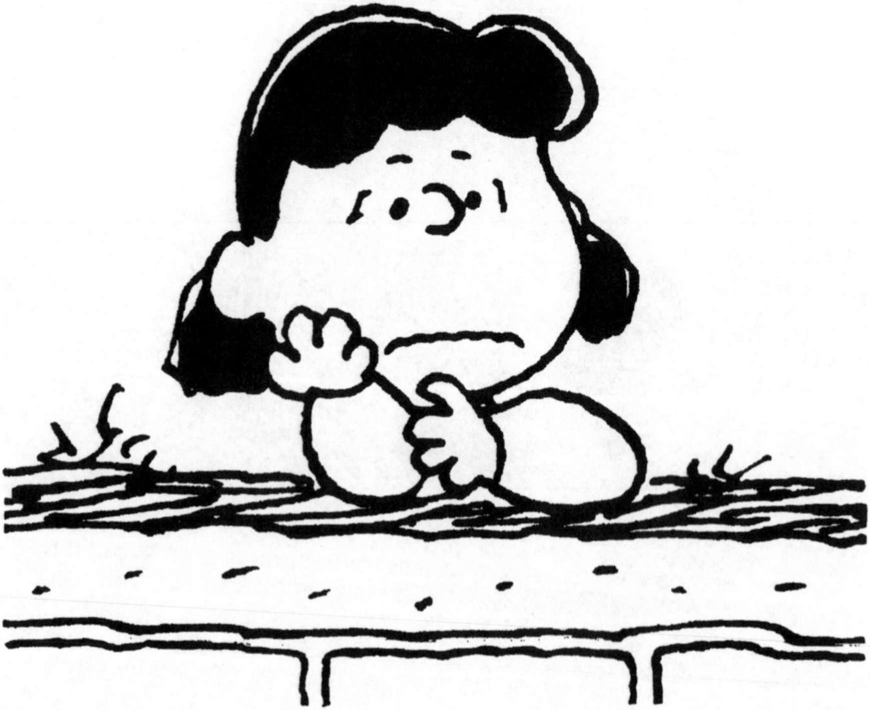

"It's amazing how stupid
you can be when you're in love . . ."

Lucy

"GIVING!
The only real joy is GIVING!"

Charlie Brown

"Love is not knowing what you're talking about."

Lucy

"When no one loves you, you have to pretend that everyone loves you!"

Sally

"Love makes you do
strange things..."

Charlie Brown

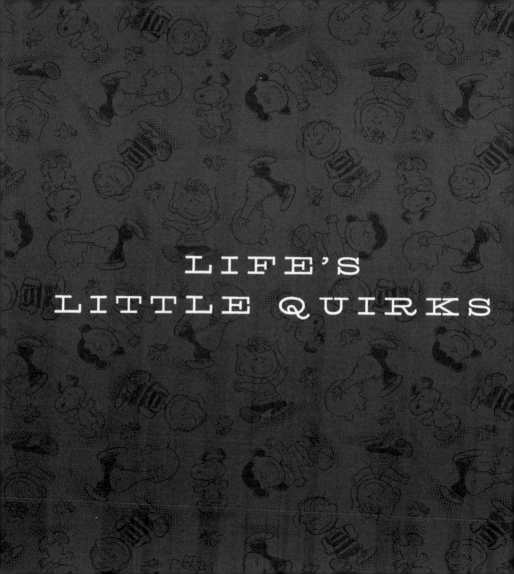

LIFE'S
LITTLE QUIRKS

HI, CHARLES..MAY I BORROW YOUR DOG FOR THE DAY ?
www.snoopy.com
YOU CAN'T BORROW A DOG.. YOU CAN BORROW MONEY, OR A BASEBALL GLOVE, OR A CAR, BUT YOU CAN'T BORROW A DOG..
6-15
I DIDN'T KNOW THAT..
© 1999 United Feature Syndicate, Inc.
SCHULZ
ASK YOUR DAD IF I CAN BORROW HIS CAR..

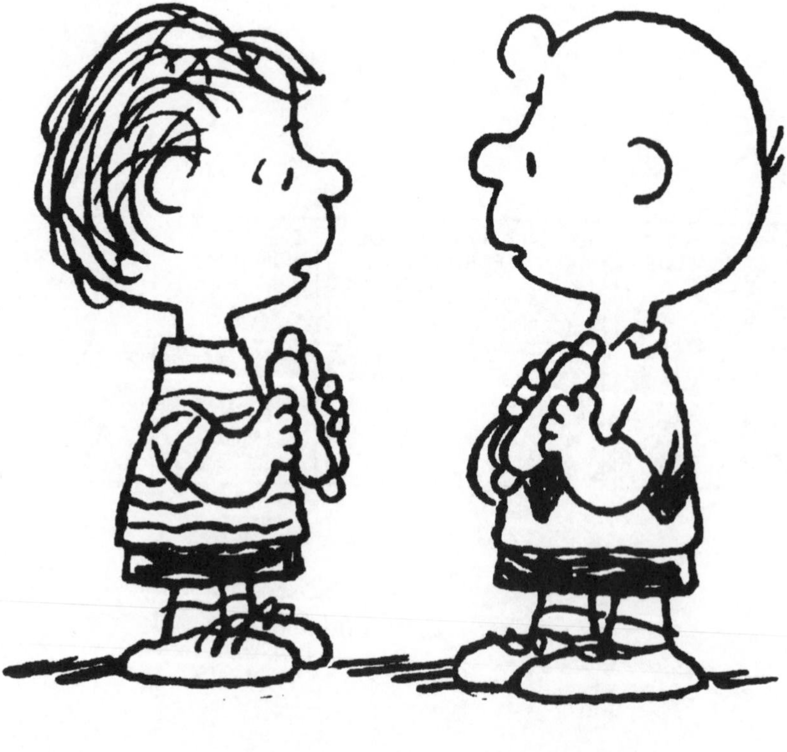

"A hot dog just doesn't taste right without a ball game in front of it!"

Charlie Brown

"That's life . . . people go away,
and dogs stay home . . ."

Charlie Brown

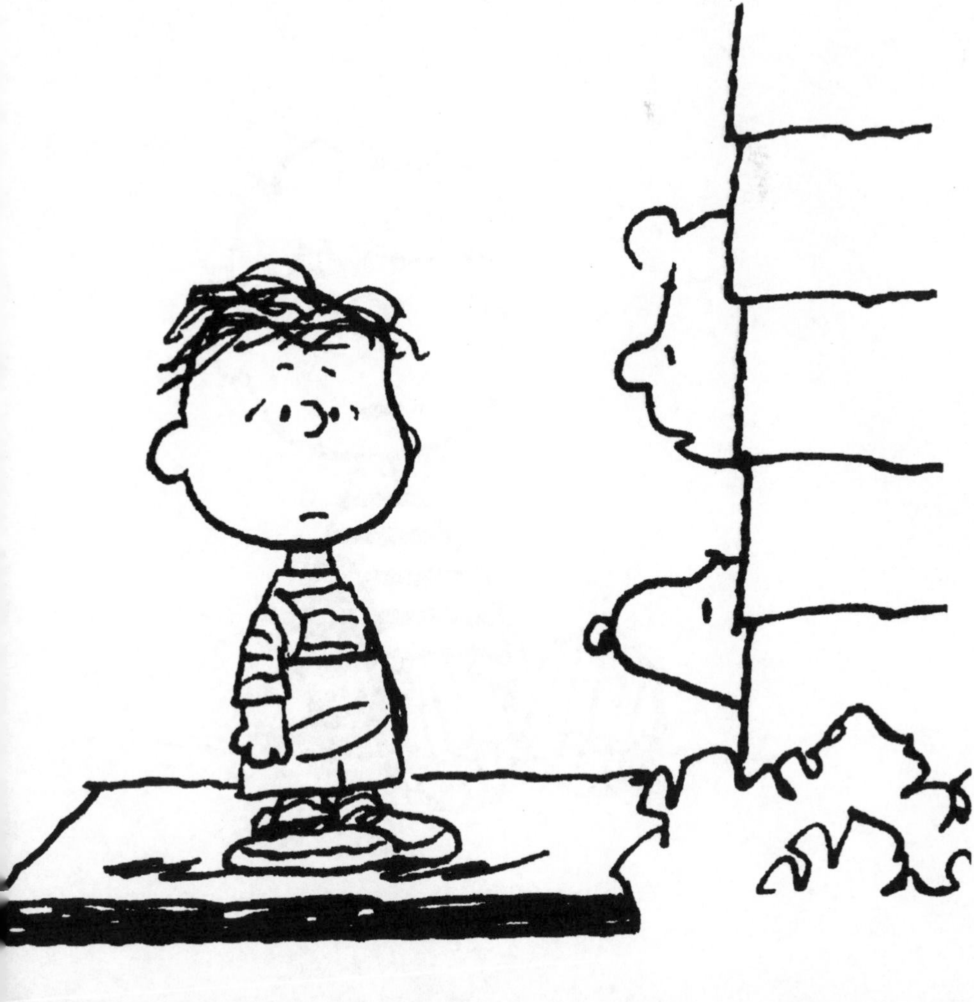

"I guess babysitters are like used cars ... you never really know what you're getting ..."

Schroeder

"A watched supper dish never fills!"

Snoopy

"There's nothing that can harm
a person more than too much
formal education!"

Linus

"It's impossible to be gloomy
when you're sitting behind
a marshmallow..."

Lucy

"Life has its sunshine and its rain, sir ... its days and its nights ... its peaks and its valleys ..."

Marcie

"In the book of life, the answers are not in the back!"

Charlie Brown